Cursive

Handwriting Workbook for Adults

By
Life Style Daily

© 2024 Life Style Daily. All rights reserved.

No part of this publication may be reproduced, distributed, or transmitted in any form or by any means, including photocopying, recording, or other electronic or mechanical methods, without the prior written permission of the publisher, except in the case of brief quotations embodied in critical reviews and certain other noncommercial uses permitted by copyright law. For permission requests, write to the publisher, addressed "Attention: Permissions Coordinator," at the address provided by Life Style Daily.

Unauthorized use and/or duplication of this material without express and written permission from Life Style Daily is strictly prohibited. Violators will be prosecuted to the fullest extent of the law.

Introduction

Welcome to the world of cursive writing—a craft that merges beauty with functionality. This book is designed to guide you step-by-step through the elegant curves and fluid connections that define cursive handwriting. Whether you are a beginner eager to explore calligraphy or someone looking to refresh and enhance your skills, you will find everything you need to embark on your journey with cursive.

While often perceived as a relic of the past, cursive writing still holds its place in the modern world. In the digital age, the ability to write beautifully by hand can set your personal and professional communications apart, adding depth and character. Additionally, learning cursive offers benefits such as improved hand-eye coordination, patience, and concentration abilities.

In this book, you will begin your journey with the basics—learning individual letters, both uppercase and lowercase. You will then progress to linking them into words and complete sentences, gradually developing your skills until you are creating full calligraphic projects that can grace greeting cards, invitations, or even personalized journals.

Prepare to be captivated by the beauty of smooth lines and elegant turns. This journey promises not just skill development but also the opportunity to express yourself in a completely new, artistic way.

So buckle up and prepare your pens—cursive awaits to be rediscovered by you.

Upper Case Elegance: Sculpting Beautiful Capitals
Trace, Repeat, Perfect: The Cursive Practice Cycle

Upper Case Elegance: Sculpting Beautiful Capitals
Trace, Repeat, Perfect: The Cursive Practice Cycle

Upper Case Elegance: Sculpting Beautiful Capitals
Trace, Repeat, Perfect: The Cursive Practice Cycle

C C C C C

C C C C C

C C C C C

C C C C C

C C C C C

Upper Case Elegance: Sculpting Beautiful Capitals
Trace, Repeat, Perfect: The Cursive Practice Cycle

Upper Case Elegance: Sculpting Beautiful Capitals
Trace, Repeat, Perfect: The Cursive Practice Cycle

E E E E E

E E E E E

E E E E E

E E E E E

E E E E E

Upper Case Elegance: Sculpting Beautiful Capitals
Trace, Repeat, Perfect: The Cursive Practice Cycle

J J J J J

J J J J J

J J J J J

J J J J J

J J J J J

Upper Case Elegance: Sculpting Beautiful Capitals

Upper Case Elegance: Sculpting Beautiful Capitals
Trace, Repeat, Perfect: The Cursive Practice Cycle

G G G G G
G G G G G
G G G G G
G G G G G
G G G G G

Upper Case Elegance: Sculpting Beautiful Capitals
Trace, Repeat, Perfect: The Cursive Practice Cycle

Upper Case Elegance: Sculpting Beautiful Capitals
Trace, Repeat, Perfect: The Cursive Practice Cycle

Upper Case Elegance: Sculpting Beautiful Capitals
Trace, Repeat, Perfect: The Cursive Practice Cycle

Upper Case Elegance: Sculpting Beautiful Capitals
Trace, Repeat, Perfect: The Cursive Practice Cycle

Upper Case Elegance: Sculpting Beautiful Capitals
Trace, Repeat, Perfect: The Cursive Practice Cycle

L L L L L

L L L L L

L L L L L

L L L L L

L L L L L

Upper Case Elegance: Sculpting Beautiful Capitals
Trace, Repeat, Perfect: The Cursive Practice Cycle

Mr   Mr   Mr   Mr   Mr

Mr   Mr   Mr   Mr   Mr

Mr   Mr   Mr   Mr   Mr

Mr   Mr   Mr   Mr   Mr

Mr   Mr   Mr   Mr   Mr

Upper Case Elegance: Sculpting Beautiful Capitals
Trace, Repeat, Perfect: The Cursive Practice Cycle

h   h   h   h   h

h   h   h   h   h

h   h   h   h   h

h   h   h   h   h

h   h   h   h   h

Upper Case Elegance: Sculpting Beautiful Capitals
Trace, Repeat, Perfect: The Cursive Practice Cycle

O O O O O

O O O O O

O O O O O

O O O O O

O O O O O

Upper Case Elegance: Sculpting Beautiful Capitals
Trace, Repeat, Perfect: The Cursive Practice Cycle

Upper Case Elegance: Sculpting Beautiful Capitals
Trace, Repeat, Perfect: The Cursive Practice Cycle

Upper Case Elegance: Sculpting Beautiful Capitals
Trace, Repeat, Perfect: The Cursive Practice Cycle

Upper Case Elegance: Sculpting Beautiful Capitals
Trace, Repeat, Perfect: The Cursive Practice Cycle

Upper Case Elegance: Sculpting Beautiful Capitals
Trace, Repeat, Perfect: The Cursive Practice Cycle

Upper Case Elegance: Sculpting Beautiful Capitals
Trace, Repeat, Perfect: The Cursive Practice Cycle

Upper Case Elegance: Sculpting Beautiful Capitals
Trace, Repeat, Perfect: The Cursive Practice Cycle

Upper Case Elegance: Sculpting Beautiful Capitals
Trace, Repeat, Perfect: The Cursive Practice Cycle

Upper Case Elegance: Sculpting Beautiful Capitals
Trace, Repeat, Perfect: The Cursive Practice Cycle

Upper Case Elegance: Sculpting Beautiful Capitals
Trace, Repeat, Perfect: The Cursive Practice Cycle

Y   Y   Y   Y   Y

Y   Y   Y   Y   Y

Y   Y   Y   Y   Y

Y   Y   Y   Y   Y

Y   Y   Y   Y   Y

Upper Case Elegance: Sculpting Beautiful Capitals
Trace, Repeat, Perfect: The Cursive Practice Cycle

Lower Case Loops: Crafting Elegant Small Letters
Trace, Repeat, Perfect: The Cursive Practice Cycle

a   a   a   a   a

a   a   a   a   a

a   a   a   a   a

a   a   a   a   a

a   a   a   a   a

Lower Case Loops: Crafting Elegant Small Letters
Trace, Repeat, Perfect: The Cursive Practice Cycle

b b b b b

b b b b b

b b b b b

b b b b b

b b b b b

Lower Case Loops: Crafting Elegant Small Letters
Trace, Repeat, Perfect: The Cursive Practice Cycle

c c c c c

c c c c c

c c c c c

c c c c c

c c c c c

Lower Case Loops: Crafting Elegant Small Letters

Trace, Repeat, Perfect: The Cursive Practice Cycle

d d d d d

d d d d d

d d d d d

d d d d d

d d d d d

Lower Case Loops: Crafting Elegant Small Letters

Trace, Repeat, Perfect: The Cursive Practice Cycle

e e e e e

e e e e e

e e e e e

e e e e e

e e e e e

Lower Case Loops: Crafting Elegant Small Letters

Lower Case Loops: Crafting Elegant Small Letters
Trace, Repeat, Perfect: The Cursive Practice Cycle

Lower Case Loops: Crafting Elegant Small Letters
Trace, Repeat, Perfect: The Cursive Practice Cycle

g g g g g

g g g g g

g g g g g

g g g g g

g g g g g

Lower Case Loops: Crafting Elegant Small Letters

Trace, Repeat, Perfect: The Cursive Practice Cycle

Lower Case Loops: Crafting Elegant Small Letters
Trace, Repeat, Perfect: The Cursive Practice Cycle

i　i　i　i　i

i　i　i　i　i

i　i　i　i　i

i　i　i　i　i

i　i　i　i　i

Lower Case Loops: Crafting Elegant Small Letters
Trace, Repeat, Perfect: The Cursive Practice Cycle

Lower Case Loops: Crafting Elegant Small Letters

Trace, Repeat, Perfect: The Cursive Practice Cycle

k   k   k   k   k

k   k   k   k   k

k   k   k   k   k

k   k   k   k   k

k   k   k   k   k

Lower Case Loops: Crafting Elegant Small Letters

Trace, Repeat, Perfect: The Cursive Practice Cycle

Lower Case Loops: Crafting Elegant Small Letters
Trace, Repeat, Perfect: The Cursive Practice Cycle

in   in   in   in   in

in   in   in   in   in

in   in   in   in   in

in   in   in   in   in

in   in   in   in   in

Lower Case Loops: Crafting Elegant Small Letters
Trace, Repeat, Perfect: The Cursive Practice Cycle

n n n n n

n n n n n

n n n n n

n n n n n

n n n n n

Lower Case Loops: Crafting Elegant Small Letters
Trace, Repeat, Perfect: The Cursive Practice Cycle

o   o   o   o   o

o   o   o   o   o

o   o   o   o   o

o   o   o   o   o

o   o   o   o   o

Lower Case Loops: Crafting Elegant Small Letters
Trace, Repeat, Perfect: The Cursive Practice Cycle

p   p   p   p   p

p   p   p   p   p

p   p   p   p   p

p   p   p   p   p

p   p   p   p   p

Lower Case Loops: Crafting Elegant Small Letters

Trace, Repeat, Perfect: The Cursive Practice Cycle

Lower Case Loops: Crafting Elegant Small Letters
Trace, Repeat, Perfect: The Cursive Practice Cycle

Lower Case Loops: Crafting Elegant Small Letters
Trace, Repeat, Perfect: The Cursive Practice Cycle

Lower Case Loops: Crafting Elegant Small Letters
Trace, Repeat, Perfect: The Cursive Practice Cycle

t t t t t

t t t t t

t t t t t

t t t t t

t t t t t

Lower Case Loops: Crafting Elegant Small Letters
Trace, Repeat, Perfect: The Cursive Practice Cycle

u u u u u

u u u u u

u u u u u

u u u u u

u u u u u

Lower Case Loops: Crafting Elegant Small Letters

Lower Case Loops: Crafting Elegant Small Letters
Trace, Repeat, Perfect: The Cursive Practice Cycle

Lower Case Loops: Crafting Elegant Small Letters
Trace, Repeat, Perfect: The Cursive Practice Cycle

Lower Case Loops: Crafting Elegant Small Letters
Trace, Repeat, Perfect: The Cursive Practice Cycle

Lower Case Loops: Crafting Elegant Small Letters
Trace, Repeat, Perfect: The Cursive Practice Cycle

Lower Case Loops: Crafting Elegant Small Letters
Trace, Repeat, Perfect: The Cursive Practice Cycle

z z z z z

z z z z z

z z z z z

z z z z z

z z z z z

Link It Up:
Cursive Letter Combinations

An An An An An

Th Th Th Th Th

In In In In In

Or Or Or Or Or

Al Al Al Al Al

En En En En En

Re Re Re Re Re

Es Es Es Es Es

On On On On On

Link It Up:
Cursive Letter Combinations

Ly Ly Ly Ly Ly

Er Er Er Er Er

Is Is Is Is Is

Co Co Co Co Co

Me Me Me Me Me

It It It It It

Ou Ou Ou Ou Ou

Ea Ea Ea Ea Ea

Ar Ar Ar Ar Ar

Word Crafting:
Building Skills with Cursive Words

Ask Ask Ask Ask

Blue Blue Blue Blue

Child Child Child

Dream Dream Dream

Earth Earth Earth

Flower Flower Flower

Garden Garden Garden

Happy Happy Happy

Island Island Island

Word Crafting:
Building Skills with Cursive Words

Joyful   Joyful   Joyful

Kitten   Kitten   Kitten

Light   Light   Light

Morning   Morning

Night   Night   Night

Orange   Orange   Orange

Peace   Peace   Peace   Peace

Quiet   Quiet   Quiet   Quiet

River   River   River   River

Smooth Scripting:
Fluid Exercises for Cursive Writing

Love conquers all

Time heals everything

Dream big dreams

Less is more

Strength in unity

Peace begins with smile

Change is constant

Hope anchors the soul

Joy in simplicity

Smooth Scripting:
Fluid Exercises for Cursive Writing

Truth prevails always

Never stop exploring

Creativity takes courage

Act without expectation

Life is beautiful

Gratitude is key

Dare to dream

Seek the truth

Laugh every day

Smooth Scripting:
Fluid Exercises for Cursive Writing

Trust the process

Keep moving forward

Cherish every moment

Follow your heart

Stay curious always

Embrace the unknown

Spread the love

Live, laugh, love

Be the change

Smooth Scripting:
Fluid Exercises for Cursive Writing

Hold the vision

Trust your intuition

Joy follows kindness

Grow through life

Love life fully

Chase your dreams

Speak your truth

Hope over fear

Stay strong always

Smooth Scripting:
Fluid Exercises for Cursive Writing

Rise above the storm

Find peace within

Create lasting memories

Live with purpose

Choose joy daily

Imagine and achieve

Celebrate small victories

Believe in magic

Harmony brings happiness

Smooth Scripting:
Fluid Exercises for Cursive Writing

Walk with confidence

Learn from yesterday

Embrace new beginnings

Dream without fear

Lead with kindness

Share your vision

Savor life's sweetness

Nurture your soul

Inspire and motivate

Composing Cursive: Sentences and Paragraphs

The morning breeze refreshes my soul.

Every adventure requires a first step.

Laughter is the sound of the soul dancing.

Books are the keys to your imagination.

Composing Cursive: Sentences and Paragraphs

Music can heal wounds which medicine cannot touch.

True friends walk in when the rest of the world walks out.

Every moment is a fresh beginning.

Composing Cursive: Sentences and Paragraphs

Silence speaks when words can't. Adventure may hurt you but monotony will kill you. Change your thoughts and you change your world. Nothing is permanent except change.

Composing Cursive: Sentences and Paragraphs

Kindness is a language which the deaf can hear and the blind can see.

Failure is the condiment that gives success its flavor.

Every sunrise is an invitation to brighten someone's day.

Patience is the art of hoping without despairing.

Crafting Occasion Cards:
Personal Touches with Cursive

Christmas Card:

Merry Christmas! May this magical season fill your heart with joy, and the coming year bring you only happiness.

Crafting Occasion Cards: Personal Touches with Cursive

Merry Christmas!

Crafting Occasion Cards: Personal Touches with Cursive

Mother's Day Card:

Dear Mom,
Thank you for your love and warmth that are with me every day. Wishing you the happiest Mother's Day!

Crafting Occasion Cards: Personal Touches with Cursive

Dear Mom,

Crafting Occasion Cards: Personal Touches with Cursive

Valentine's Day Card:

To My Valentine,
With each day, my love for you grows stronger. Valentine's Day is every day since you are with me.

Crafting Occasion Cards:
Personal Touches with Cursive

To My Valentine,

Crafting Occasion Cards: Personal Touches with Cursive

Birthday Card:

Happy Birthday!
May this year be full of health, joy, and the fulfillment of all your dreams.
Best birthday wishes!

Crafting Occasion Cards:
Personal Touches with Cursive

Happy Birthday!

Crafting Occasion Cards: Personal Touches with Cursive

Easter Card:

Happy Easter! May your day be filled with joy, peace, and the warmth of family and friends.

Crafting Occasion Cards:
Personal Touches with Cursive

Happy Easter!

Crafting Occasion Cards:
Personal Touches with Cursive

Father's Day Card:

Dear Dad,
Thank you for your strength and guidance. Wishing you a very Happy Father's Day!

Crafting Occasion Cards:
Personal Touches with Cursive

Dear Dad,

Crafting Occasion Cards:
Personal Touches with Cursive

Thanksgiving Card:

Happy Thanksgiving! Grateful for the wonderful times we share and the memories we make together.

Crafting Occasion Cards: Personal Touches with Cursive

Happy Thanksgiving!

Crafting Occasion Cards:
Personal Touches with Cursive

New Year's Card:

Happy New Year! Wishing you a year filled with new adventures, successes, and happiness.

Crafting Occasion Cards: Personal Touches with Cursive

Happy New Year!

Days of the Week in Cursive

Monday Monday

Tuesday Tuesday Tuesday

Wednesday Wednesday

Thursday Thursday

Friday Friday Friday

Saturday Saturday

Sunday Sunday Sunday

Months of the Year in Cursive

January January

February February

March March March

April April April

May May May May

June June June June

July July July July

August August August

September September

Months of the Year in Cursive

October October October

November November

December December

Numbers in Cursive

Zero Zero Zero Zero

One One One One One

Two Two Two Two Two

Three Three Three Three

Four Four Four Four

Five Five Five Five

Six Six Six Six Six Six

Seven Seven Seven

Eight Eight Eight

Numbers in Cursive

Nine Nine Nine Nine

0 0 0 0 0 0 0 0 0

1 1 1 1 1 1 1 1 1 1

2 2 2 2 2 2 2 2 2 2

3 3 3 3 3 3 3 3 3 3

4 4 4 4 4 4 4 4 4 4

5 5 5 5 5 5 5 5 5 5

6 6 6 6 6 6 6 6 6 6

7 7 7 7 7 7 7 7 7 7

Numbers in Cursive

Final Reflections

As we close the pages of this workbook, I hope you have discovered the timeless beauty and practical elegance that cursive writing offers. Throughout these chapters, we have explored the curves and connections that define this art form—from mastering each letter to linking them into words and sentences, and finally applying them in real-world projects.

Cursive writing is more than just a method of communication; it is a bridge to our past and a tool for future expression. It connects us to history, to the personal touch that electronic communication cannot convey, and to a mindfulness in writing that is meditative and deliberate. Continue to practice what you have learned here. The journey to cursive mastery is a path of continuous improvement and enjoyment.

Seek out new projects, incorporate cursive into your daily life—whether through journaling, crafting personalized gifts, or simply sending handwritten notes to friends and family.

Remember, the nuances of your personal style will emerge more prominently the more you write. Each stroke you make not only improves your technique but also helps forge a deeper connection with your words.

This personal touch is what makes cursive an enduring art form.

Thank you for choosing this workbook as your guide. May your continued practice bring you not only improved skill but also a greater appreciation for the written word. Carry forward the grace and fluidity of cursive writing into all aspects of your written expression.

As you move forward, let each pen stroke express not just words, but a part of your very soul. Write passionately, write creatively, and most importantly, write yourself into the pages of the world.

www.ingramcontent.com/pod-product-compliance
Lightning Source LLC
LaVergne TN
LVHW060335080526
838202LV00053B/4480